I0470275

CONTENTS

DEDICATION

◆ ◆ ◆

This 2nd part of the, "How To Get Your Money Back ... And Then Some," series is dedicated once again to my children. Life has so many unexpected twists and turns. You can plan all you want, but only the Lord knows how it will unfold. This 2nd part is for you to learn how to react when your golden plan doesn't go the way you wanted it to. Keep your head up. Keep fighting the good fight. I love you all.

This 2nd part is also for anyone else who lives a life that has thrown you to your knees, or lifted you to the heights unexpectedly and then punished you later down the road with a taxation curve ball. Nothing the world gives seems to truly be free. The current taxation system punishes you for making more money, and then audits those that make hardly any. If you have found yourself at either end, or approaching these paths, then this is for you.

Thank you, Lord, for teaching me how to roll with the punches. You're always a thousand steps ahead, and all I need to do is follow in Your footsteps. Thank You for being a constant light unto my path and a lamp unto my feet. I love you.

◆ ◆ ◆

PREFACE

◆ ◆ ◆

Side Note:

This is not a book about legal advice for your individual financial concerns. This book is only my experiences and should not be taken as more than that and should not be generalized to more than myself. Please see a lawyer, CPA, or both for personal legal advice. I am not responsible for any decisions that others make with their finances. Again, this book is only my personal experiences. Thank you.

I hope you have read *Part 1* of the series, *How To Get Your Money Back... And Then Some*, and for all intents and purposes I will assume you have. If you haven't, go check it out! It's vital for understanding this book. This book summarizes what each person can do in a year's time to ensure that they have done the best they can do to avoid paying any taxes, legally, and to even have the government pay you for living here as well. I shared my failures in the last book- I'll share in this book how I actively made a present change to overcome in 2018 and 2019 and onward. I hope that it makes you see everything differently, and gives you hope. Please don't feel guilty or ashamed or embarrassed if you've found yourself in a similar place that I've been. Let it go and move on. So let's get to it then!

RECALLING MY STORY

◆ ◆ ◆

This is a quick snap shot of where I was financially in 2018. This is from an excerpt of my first book:

"I graduated from college with a Bachelor's of Science in Mathematics and Chemistry. Thankfully, the Lord taught me about hard work and favor, and my time during undergraduate college was paid for by the government since I did well in high school. Then I went to get my doctorate at Shenandoah

University. 3 years later, I was a $250,000 (1/4 a million)-in-debt Doctor... This was not exactly what I was hoping for.

What welcomed me after graduation was my best friend: anxiety. I started to have panic attacks about how much I owed, and how long I would have to work to pay it off, and what would happen if I didn't pay my monthly payments. *What else could they take? I didn't **have** anything else.* I rented a home with friends, leased a car from my parents for free (who also graciously paid my car insurance), and I had nothing saved up. I quickly realized that I **had** to work. I was officially enslaved to my job. There was no other way getting around it. Or so I thought.

But before I learned what the solution was, I made my financial problems much worse. It wasn't like I intentionally meant to. But being unaware of the taxation system cost me much more than what I ever thought it would- money, time, health, and it almost cost me my marriage. After I got my first official job, I was still single and had no real payments besides my student loan monthly amount. I therefore tried to pay down my student loans as quickly as possible, I ate well, and I traveled often on vacations around the world, usually performing mission work every chance I could. If I had extra money, I gave it away. But this left me with nothing saved up for my first 2 years.

My boss at the time introduced me to the IRA system, which he stated he would contribute up to a certain percentage of what I contributed. Free money?! This sounded amazing. And it is, when done correctly. Unfortunately, after multiple confrontations later, it was obvious he had knowingly NOT contributed his amount, AND had also NOT fully put in my amount. I don't know why I never reported it, because it was stealing at its finest. I was probably too embarrassed. I was working for a great company. Everyone was so nice. How could this have ever happened to me? But those were just excuses.

Anyway, 2 years later, I never thought I would get married. And then I got married.

I unfortunately had a very fancy wedding in D.C. in 2017 and decided to buy the hotel rooms for all the guests. While it was nice at the time, I think I went just a little overboard with wedding planning. And by little, **I mean goodbye $30,000.** The wedding was planned for D.C. so that Anna's family and friends could fly in. Unfortunately, the U.S. denied all their requests to come, even her parents, about a month before our wedding date. I don't know why I didn't just cancel the venue and move it to a less expensive place in Winchester, VA. But I didn't.

So how did I come up with the money? Easy. Credit cards, the money saved in my IRA account, and my biweekly paychecks for that month of January. **This left me $14,000 dollars in credit card debt.** Oh, and not to mention all the stress. I really started my marriage off well (sarcasm). Poor Anna. Don't worry. It only continued to get worse.

I decided the only way out of this was to work more, spend less, and decrease all debt. This seemed to work for some people.

Famous Christians have written so many books about the success in doing this. I was sure it would work for me, too. However, when I tried to cut expenses, I realized we had already been doing this. We had one car which was used, no T.V., no internet, hardly any furniture, we utilized coupons, had no monthly subscriptions, and only rewarded ourselves with eating out occasionally (all of which are still true statements). I then decided to get an additional job that paid significantly more to increase my income.

However, this led to the main event that further catalyzed my financial mess, though it was not my employer's fault. The business had decided to switch me to an independent contractor in 2017, as they had done to everyone else as well. I didn't really have any say. I just let it happen. I didn't know what it meant, and I didn't bother to look it up. I switched to a full-time position at the end of 2016, which carried on in 2017. I made a little over $90,000 total for 2017. It was the most profitable year I had ever experienced. Or so I had thought. All of the driving for my job in home health forced me into buying a better used vehicle, with trading in the previous used vehicle. **Add another $10,000 in debt via auto loan. Credit card usage however was starting to lower, with it being around $5,000.**

It was at this point Anna and I decided to plan on having a baby. However, we needed to move. Instead of going to a different home and renting, I decided to buy a home. I had heard that there were numerous financial benefits in owning a home, so I thought now was the time (two weeks before my 1st child was due). We found an amazing townhome, which we still live in, and bought this in January 22, 2018. Yet unfortunately, we hardly use 1/2 of the space (we are in an active plan to change this). I used an FHA loan for this, and got sucker punched x 2 with PMI, which I didn't fully understand at the time. **After giving away $3,000 dollars to the government for free, owing my parents $8000 for the down payment, and being $5,000 dollars in additional credit card debt from the home purchase, we moved**

into our home. *Is this what it feels like to be a homeowner*? 2 weeks later, my baby was born. And we were blessed with an insanely amazing healthy baby girl, but completely unaware of the costs, even with health insurance. **I was easily another $5000 dollars in debt for the baby via credit cards. The next day after my baby was born, I went back to work. Commitment, some would call it. Slavery is what it really was.**

Just to recap, at this point I was **$125,000 in debt for student loans, $20,000 in debt in credit card usage, $10,000 in debt for the car, $8000 in debt to my parents for the house, $3,000 gone to the government for the house, and had a $1,400 mortgage monthly payment** (includes real estate tax, PMI, HOA, home owners insurance). What a way to start the marriage. Don't worry, again it only got worse.

After my baby was born in February 5, 2018, I thought that completing my taxes for 2017 would at least give me some needed financial support. Unfortunately, it gave me the opposite. **I owed the government $17,000.** I'm not even making this up. I just didn't know what it meant to be an independent contractor. And I paid for it. Literally. Prior to this, I had gotten a small refund every year. 2017 changed everything.

As my stress increased with the addition of a baby with jaundice and a traumatized wife from a complicated birthing process, I had no idea what to do. I did what every person likely does in moments of chaos- I googled and freaked out. I know I should have sought the Lord and asked for wise counsel, but I didn't. Websites arose with the slogan "personal loan" and I was immediately captivated. I didn't realize an unsecured loan aka "personal loan" has significantly higher APR. I thought I was grabbing a deal for a $27,500 loan with 12.20 % APR.

I distributed the personal loan to the federal tax of $17,000, gave $6000 towards the car, and then sent the rest to the credit cards. I worked extremely hard and was able to get the total credit card usage down to

$5000 by the end of the year. This left me with the following: **$110,000 in student loan debt, $27,500 in personal loan debt, $8,000 in debt to my parents, $5,000 in credit card debt, $2,500 in car debt (totaling $153,000), and monthly payments for the home, student loans, personal loan, car, adding up to around $2,400 per month**.

This significantly lowered my credit score into the 690's. It was the lowest it had ever been. And maybe one of the lowest points for me as well. I was now officially living paycheck to paycheck. One paycheck would go to my monthly payments. The other would go to food, the water bill, electricity bill, and gas. The small remainder would go towards the credit card debt. No savings. No emergency fund.

The personal loan had only bought me some time. I was so scared to owe money to the IRS that I couldn't even pay, and shocked that I was *that* person. I didn't want to go to jail. No, thanks. So, my only option was just to work harder and cut out any additional expenses as much as possible. I tried to get multiple jobs as I became extremely depressed and borderline suicidal. It was a horrific time. I just thought *if I work more, I'll get out of this*. And that's what people think... for 50 years of their life. And then they retire, and think the government/family/fairy godmother will take care of them. I was going to be one of those people, forever enslaved to the job. The only problem was... I had a wife and a child. I had huge dreams. And I was not going to compromise on letting my family drown or allowing my dreams to die. So, I left my narrow-mind by the door along with any remaining pride and asked the Lord for help. And oh, did He answer."

HOW I GOT OUT, PRACTICALLY

◆ ◆ ◆

The first thing I did was **1) pray.** I needed wisdom (which in Greek is Sophia, which conveniently enough is our daughter's name). So why not go to the One who has all the wisdom, and where wisdom started. It gave me peace to know that God didn't condemn me for where I was, but offered His open hand to pull me out of the pit, as He always does. I had someone on my side, that wasn't in the pit. This was so comforting. Anxiety can really play with the mind and it's so hard to think clearly when it clouds your every thought.

2) I Decreased Expenses.

After receiving peace, here is what I did to move on and get out from a practical standpoint. I first **decreased my expenses**. I **lowered my car insurance payment** by lowering the coverage amount. This dropped it 50% per month. **I increased our home owner's insurance policy deductible**, which lowered our home insurance monthly cost by 13.7%. I **stopped our internet** at our townhome and **started going to the local coffee shop**, Hopscotch Coffee and Records, to do my documentation. Amazing house coffee + tip = $2.00 with free internet access, and the 8th cup is free. I don't know how you can beat that. 20 weekdays in a month – 2 freebies, equals $36.00. At home, my internet bill was $50.00 per month without free coffee. We live about 1 mile away from the shop, so gas is not an issue. This just makes financial sense. I was losing

$14.00 per month before changing to this plan. **I changed our phone bill** to maximize our usage of data and to not be penalized for going overboard. I **stopped my kick-boxing membership** ($150.00 per month) and **started working out at home in my free time**. I **quit drinking Coke** (which varied from $1.50-2.50 per drink) and **started drinking water** (which is usually always free). I **started to eat at home more often than eating out** (this part was the hardest, but my wife is a phenomenally patient cook!). And **when I did eat out, I chose a singular restaurant that participated in a rewards program that offered free food as a redeemable option, Chick Fil-A.**

My wife immediately came on board and started grocery shopping even more wisely, looking for **sales and coupons**. She then stopped us from using our electric dryer and instead utilized **air drying through the old-fashioned technique of clothes-lines and hangers**. This saved us at least $50 per month on our electricity bill. **She would walk to work when possible**, which would also decrease our gas consumption, and ensure she got her exercise in for the day.

3) I increased my time available.

I did this by **decreasing my radius of work**, meaning I would only see patients in the Winchester area. I quit going as much to Front Royal, Woodstock, Gore, so I didn't have the driving time wasted anymore. I would only go to those places when treating multiple patients in an assisted living facility, which would cut my drive time in half. This allowed me to get my work done much more quickly and **allowed me to stop and think**. This was so crucial, because if one doesn't have the time free to think, no change can ever be made. I took a pay cut initially, but got it all back in the end because I became more efficient. The allure of driving a longer distance for a higher paying job in my opinion may not be all it's cracked up to be. I found that I had less stress, and more free time, and it caused me to become creative. I could get more involved in my local community because I was home more often. And I could be involved in my grow-ing family. Priceless.

4) I then sold the limited valuables that I had not been using that were not incredibly personal to my wife or myself.

Furniture? Goodbye. My Guitar? Gone. Suit-cases? Bye. Books from School? No more. We got rid of our mattress and got an air mat-tress, as it's portable. **We kept Anna's wed-ding dress and didn't touch anything that Sophia had. I didn't want my daughter or my wife to be punished for my ill choices.** So-phia had more clothes and things than Anna and I both combined (this is still true). It's hard to see things go that you once enjoyed. But then it gave me a fight to one day get to the place where I can be financially stable to get them back, without the stress engraved within them.

5) Next, I learned the value of shifting debt.

The goal was to put the most interest-bear-ing debt into a holding place to be left for a time. This is incredibly essential to becoming debt-free. My most interest-bearing debt was my credit card usage. **I put all my credit card debt onto one credit card with 0% APR for 15 months with 0% balance transfer fee**. This meant I didn't have to worry about that debt accruing interest for 15 months, because that's a losing battle that no one needs to fight. This freed me up with more money available to put where I needed it the most. I then limited usage to only that particular card. Traveling less and eating out less decreased my credit card usage dramatically.

6) I then prioritized my debt.

I **focused on the most important debt apart from credit car usage**. Many people focus on student loans and the urgency to repay them as soon as possible. This is a huge mistake. If one simply applies for the repayment method, the government can only take up to 10% of your check every month, and then promises to forgive your loan in 20 years for undergraduate or 25 years for graduate loans. Usually they don't even do the maximum 10% monthly payment. I went from owing the government $650 to $218 a month. In 25 years, the government will theoretically pay off my loan for me.

Let's look at this calculation. $218/month x 12 months/1 year x 25 years = $65,400 paid by me. My total amount currently for my student loans is about $100,000. However, most people will try to pay this off in a few years, with interest accruing. I would save at least $34,600 of my own money if I had the government do it for me.

But then it gets better. The government rewards you with a taxation benefit for having student loans and paying off interest up to a certain point. You are granted up to $2,500/year above the line deduction off of your earned income that is not subject to federal income tax. This might not seem like much, but if you extrapolate this for 25 years under a normal W-2 employee, the government has given you an approximate extra deduction of $62,500. 15.75% taxation (minimum 10% federal income + 5.75% state income tax) of $62,500 is **$9,844 of real taxes that you would not have to pay over 25 years.** $65,400 - $9,844 = $55,556. This is the corrected maximum total amount you would have paid on your student loans in 25 years. The goal is to pay off exactly $2,500 of interest-only every year in student loans. But doing more than this is not beneficial. This goes for any graduate student loan. Undergraduate is even better.

So, if you have student loans with total summation greater than $55,556, think twice about focusing on getting rid of this gem. You're missing it if you do. **This should be your last focus concerning debt.** Because I needed some room to breathe, I asked for a temporary forbearance. This gave me 3 months where I did not have to pay any monthly payment, and did not decrease my on-time payment perfect record, therefore not affecting my credit score.

I do want to make it clear at this point, that even after saying the benefit of gov-

ernment loan forgiveness, I would not rely on the government to pay off any student loans. In fact, really I think we all should all pay off our own individual loans, since we signed up for it ourselves voluntarily. *What am I saying, though, is to save this debt for the last thing you tackle.*

7) Then it was so important to pay off as much debt as possible through amending my taxes.

My personal loan was really first on the list, with 12% monthly interest rate. There was no way I could shift this to a holding cell. I needed to tackle this head on. I therefore **amended my previous taxes** for years 2015-2017, filed 2018, amended 2018, and got back $23,000, which put a significant dent into the loan of $26,500. I will talk about how I did this in likely the last addition of this series next year. The goal was then to continue to work and pay off the remaining $3,500 through earned income. Goodbye evil personal loan. I won't be missing you.

8) I then took a serious look into my "assets."

My house – the main jewel that I own- was supposed to be a tax haven. Then the Standard Deduction went up to $24,400 for 2019. This meant that having a house was no longer beneficial for taxation purposes, unless one plans on paying mortgage interest totaling > $24,400 per year. You get a deduction on the mortgage interest – not principal – that you pay for the full year. Please note that this does NOT include PMI, which is on any loan that doesn't have 80% put down. Of course, I had PMI with my FHA loan. None of that was deductible. This meant I was wasting $1,400/month x 12 months/1 year = $16,800. This includes HOA, HOI, real estate taxes, mortgage, home warranty. Anna and I could have **rented a home** in the area for $1,000/month x 12 months = $12,000, without the headache of having to fix any problems or deal with any issues. Please note that I am not blaming my realtors – we bought the house before the new tax law came into effect, and the housing market was booming and was a seller's market. This just shows how unpredictable the current taxation system is, as well as the economy.

So what do you do when the housing market tanks and you realize your jewel is now a clouded diamond? You **rent out your home**. Anna and I are renting our home out to good tenants, hopefully for 4-7 years. After that time, we desire to be at a place financially where we can gift it to Anna's charity, *Bloom The Desert*, for women in crisis. Given the housing market, we will profit at least $175/month after covering our entire housing payment, personal property taxes, insurance, warranty, home owner's association, etc. Regarding the HOA, I then **talked to the HOA president to ask for a lowered amount of yearly dues.** He seems to be agreeable with this, but we won't find out the result until later this year.

So this should have you questioning – where will I be living? Anna and I plan on going to medical school in August, as previously mentioned in the last book. The medical school costs will be covered by **scholarships** and some governmental loans, which will take care of housing costs as well. I am continuing to apply for other scholarships to attempt to further decrease my use of governmental loans.

The last "asset" to discuss is the automobile payment for our Jeep Patriot. We have two options with this- we can sell the car, which would pay off the loan and help us to pocket some cash, which would alleviate some headache. Or we can use earned income to take the loan out easily since I have only $2,500 left to pay, and we can **rent the car out**. This would allow us to potentially make some money every month. We won't be using it hardly anyway from August-May, so why not make some money on the side?

This leaves us only with **credit card debt**, which is held in a purgatory like state for 15 months. I expect to be around $9,000 in credit card debt by May 2020. However,

I will be having the **government pay me *at least* $10,000 to live here when I file my taxes in February 2020.** I therefore will use the **2020 tax return** to cover the credit card debt and then save the rest!

This plan therefore has taken care of the all debts, reduced my expenses, and help me to live more conscientious of where my money is going. However, this practically covers my past failures. What about living in the present? I'm so glad you asked...

HOW I STAYED
OUT, PRACTICALLY

◆ ◆ ◆

The first important thing to note is the necessity for financial planning for the year AND **throughout the year**. If you HAVE to pay taxes, then at least know WHY and HOW MUCH you are expecting to have to pay, that way you can set that aside. I should not have pay any taxes based upon my personal financial strategy. AND I have multiple resources and avenues to walk down if something unexpected happens in order to ensure 0 taxation remains true. That means that I don't have to worry about the final result when I file. Here is my financial strategy for years 2019 and on:

1) Pray

2) Earned income needs to be between $24,400 to $26,900

3) Personal investment income must be less than $3,600

4) All possible income and expenses must be held under independent contractor/small business owner status

5) Decrease SE/FICA taxation, legally

6) Passive business investment income needs to be constantly growing

7) Unsecured personal loans should never be taken out

8) Credit cards should be paid off every month

9) Debit card usage should increase for specific categories

10) Never buy a new car

That's it. This will ensure that I get paid by the government, which would offset all FICA tax, and end up paying $0 total in taxes, invest all along the way, and ensure early retirement occurs.

Now let's talk about why each point matters and what to do to make each point happen. The first step is to never say "This isn't going to work," or "This will never happen." These statements just invite failure and defeat into every person's life. Instead, the statement should be, "God, how can we make this happen?" And then the floodgates will open. You would be foolish to not ask for wisdom in a time of need. If God is the creator of wisdom, then it would be equally foolish to not ask God for help and advice. Hence the most important #1 strategy - **PRAY.** He is always present and always willing to help you out, especially in every need and any situation. There's never something too small or too big in your life that God doesn't care about it. He cares about everything you do. He loves you.

2) Earned income needs to be between $24,400 to $26,900.

The main reason this is so important is to be eligible for the **Earned Income Tax Credit**, which at $24,400 earned income is maxed out at $5,716 for my situation personally (Married Filing Jointly with 2 children). This is free money that the federal government will be giving me through the federal income taxation avenue. As the earned income increases at this point, the tax credit inversely starts to decrease. So why would I not just make sure that I get under $24,400 for my federal income? Because the **IRS tends to audit those that make over $200,000 per year and those that make less than $24,400 per year**. Unfortunately, there have been cases where people have stolen SSNs of children and claimed them on their taxes in order to get a financial credit from the IRS. Clearly this is illegal. However, I find it important regardless to stay out of the cross-hares of the IRS, even though I'm not doing anything illegal.

However, I could face taxation via federal income tax and state income tax if my AGI is greater than $24,400. Therefore, my goal is to end up at exactly $24,400. The way to legally make this happen is to use above the line deductions, such as the **student loan interest deduction**. Therefore, my earned income can be a maximum of $26,900 and then I take off the maximum allowed $2,500 for student loan interest deduction, which leaves me with $24,400 AGI, which means zero federal income and state taxation as this is the standard deduction. I am left with 7.65% FICA of $26,900, which is $2,058. The EITC for $26,900 is still around $5,000, which is significantly greater than the FICA tax, leaving me with a refund. I have therefore obtained the EITC, avoided all taxation, and decreased my risk of IRS auditing, legally.

The last benefit of having earned income around this range is the benefit of being **eligible for medicaid health insurance and other government subsidies**. If a family is not eligible for medicaid, they would likely get a **substantial premium tax credit on their monthly health insurance premium**, which would knock off hundreds of dollars every month, only further increasing the savings. In fact, for a married couple with children, if earned income is around 100% of the Federal Poverty Income, the federal government will essentially **pay for your entire premium amount** through the affordable healthcare website.

One of the main government subsidies you can also utilize is **WIC (Women, Infant, Children) organization,** which gives a certain amount of free groceries per month. This is a great way to decrease your grocery bill and eat more at home if you're in a financial bind. We did this for one month when Anna wasn't able to work at the end of her pregnancy, and got assisted with close to $50 for groceries for that month. After Anna was able to get back to work, we immediately stopped WIC services and thanked them for their support.

At this point, many investors start to say that their **lenders won't allow them to purchase a home with such a low AGI. This isn't true.** If your debt to income ratio is low and you have the funds saved up, then you should have no problem, as they not only look at consistent employment and debt to income ratio, but especially **monthly income**. As a small business owner or independent contractor, your yearly AGI divided by 12 months should never be the same as your monthly income (before expenses). Your monthly income should always be as high as you can get it. Conversely, you would want your AGI/12 months to be as close as possible to the number 24,400 to ensure $0 overall taxation. This would certainly allow you to snag a great mortgage, along with consistent employment > 2 years and low debt to income ratio, all without having a moderate or high AGI, all while avoiding taxation liability.

So how do you get your earned income to be so low? You either work very little through-out the year under a standard W2 job (not recommended) or you work tiresomely throughout the year under a standard W2 job that doesn't pay you hardly anything (not recommended). And that's it.

Just kidding. Here is the wise answer: **you utilize your tax-friendly outlets** to help as-sist you in meeting this goal, with you try-ing to make as much money as you can every month. Please see Part 1 of this series for further in depth explanation. In a brief sum-mary, here are the biggest ways to decrease your earned income if you are a W2-em-ployee: **contribute the maximum amount to your employer-offered 401K, contribute maximum amount to your FSA, contribute maximum amount for your HSA**.

If you are not a W2-employee, then: **you should be a small business owner, you should have your job contract out to your** business, you should write off as many expenses as you legally can, and then contribute as much as you need to in your solo 401K up to the point where, after expenses, you are at $24,400. It is much, much easier to get your earned income legally lower with being an independent contractor or small business owner than being a W2-employee.

This is exactly what I did this year. I was making moderate money as a W2 employee. When I had reached around $26,000 for my income, **I had my employer switch to contracting out to my physical therapy business**. I basically quit under the umbrella of my W2 job, went under the umbrella of my business, and had the W2 employer pay my business first instead of me. Since I was PRN (as needed), but working a full-time case load, this was completely legal. And yet my job description didn't change. I was basically doing the same thing as before, but not having to pay taxes on any of the money I made. And here comes the most beautiful part - **it was a win-win for everyone**

involved. My W2-employer no longer had to pay the 7.65% FICA tax on everything I made. This allowed them to offer me a higher rate of reimbursement. This meant - I made more money with less time involved.

And since I own the business, I am able to do a variety of things with this money if I need to. We will talk about the significance of being an S Corporation later in this book. First, I pay out all my standard expenses. Then I give the 25% of the remaining money to my retirement SEP, as this is counted towards business expenses. **The remaining money (business net earnings) left over should be exactly $866 or less, and never greater, unless it's worth it paying self-employment tax.** This will ensure $0 taxation for me. Let me explain. I will give $433 to myself through employee wages, and then give $433 to myself through non-dividend distributions. **This will allow me to pay $0 in SE tax.** We will talk about this in a few moments. Just keep this in the back of your mind for now.

And this is how it plays out: $26,000 + $433 = $26,433 earned income. Recall the maximum $2,500 above the line student loan interest deduction and the $24,400 standard deduction = $26,900. Let's say I take out $2,033 in student loan interest. $26,433 - $26,433 = $0 taxation liability = $0 to be pay in taxes, while keeping me out of the cross-hares of the IRS. This is for me personally. If you don't have student loan debt, then that's great! You don't have to rely on the student loan interest deduction. Just make sure you contribute to your TIRA or 401K. This will allow the saver's credit. The Saver's credit is so important, because if you do have any federal income taxation liability, this will offset the tax amount dollar for dollar. This ensures $0 taxation, while promoting a great return for the EITC for lowering the earned income by 401K or 403b contributions.

3) Personal investment income must be less than $3,600.

Notice I said "personal investment income." First of all, it is very important to have personal investments. This should be on your list of things to do. But even more so than this should be business investments. That's because you won't be taxed on the income made as a business, only the profit after expenses are taken out. And then even more importantly, **if you want that golden earned income tax credit, you CANNOT make $3,600 or more off of personal investment income as of 2019 IRS guidelines**. This means if I sell my home, or my car, or any asset, and make a **combined profit of personal investment income in that year of $3,600 or greater, I am completely ineligible for the EITC**.

This is very, very important to track. You can make $3,599 and then keep your $5,700 EITC, or make one dollar more at $3,600, and lose $5,700. This kept me from selling my home, my car, and kept me out of the stock market from a personal standpoint at this time. I am now funneling money into retirement accounts and making sure that the dividends do not reach a summation of $3,600 or greater, because then it becomes very costly as I would lose the EITC. My business will be renting out my home and my car, not me. In that regard, I am avoiding personal investment income. Social security income does not count as investment account by the way.

So let's say that you're fortunate enough to have retirement accounts/stock market accounts that make dividends to combine to > $3,599. This would mean on a 5% yearly dividend return, **you would have to have at least $72,000 saved as your principal. In order for your dividend output to even match the $5,700 EITC, your principal would then have to be at least $114,000.** The average American does not have this. If you are someone so blessed to have this much saved up, then I would recommend **changing your stocks to non-dividend optional growth** until your principal reaches an amount that the estimated dividend output of 5% would far exceed the EITC and government subsidies associated with low earned income (basically: dividend income needs to be >>>> than tax benefits of low earned income).

From a personal standpoint, my family and I save about $480 per month from government subsidies covering our health insurance premiums. Yearly, that's $5,760. Add the $5,700 EITC, and that's **$11,460. For our dividend income to meet this, our investment principal would have to be at $228,000 in the stock market.** Right. I don't foresee me reaching this goal in the next 5 years, but you never know. And dividend output seems to be lowering comparatively in the last few years. This would mean your principal would have to be even higher. That's why it's so important to constantly re-evaulate your game plan based upon your circumstances and the world around you.

Let's say that you make a significant amount of money off of **rental properties** or other rental assets that is greater than $3,599 per year. This **really needs to be under your**

business account, not your personal account anyway. We will talk about more of why this is important in the next section from a taxation standpoint, but from **a legal standpoint**, this is crucial. **Your amount of liability is significantly lessened with your rental assets being under the umbrella of a limited liability company**. Though it's not a 100% sure safeguard, it will minimize significant damages that could be accrued from just one incident of misfortune. Legally, it is much more difficult to find out how much the property is worth under the business, as you can choose to not disclose this. It also very hard to trace multiple businesses back to one individual.

Therefore it would be very wise to have different businesses own different rental property. This means if you get sued for one rental property, you're less likely to have damages that would exceed your current rental property. Under a LLC, access to your personal assets is very restricted. However, this is still an option if someone is crafty enough legally, so don't think that just because you have multiple businesses under separate LLCs that you will never get your assets taken from you, because that is unfortunately not the case. **It just makes it very difficult for the normal citizen to ever be able to get to that point of access.**

4) *All possible income and expenses must be held under independent contractor/small business owner status*.

In the first part of this series, I reviewed how important it was to be a small business owner. **Filing as an independent contractor or a small business owner gives you a second layer of protection agains taxation.** You are literally treated as a completely different individual in the eyes of the IRS. The business is even given a type of SSN, called an EIN. The image that I made it to understand this is somewhat comical, but humor me and follow along. I liken this to the **Superman/Clark Kent relationship**. The Clark Kent is the exterior, who is a completely different person than the interior, with his nice suit and tie donned. He is your first line of defense, almost like a shield. All financial blows hit him first. When Clark Kent has done all he can do, then the financial blow trickles down beyond him. Underneath the fancy clothes is the extremely personal Superman- AKA you. The goal is that your exterior and shield, Clark Kent, has extinguished all the financial blows, so that nothing is left to reach you, Superman.

Likewise, taxation should be treated the same. All income needs to be covered under this outer layer so that one isn't personally taxed on the income made. **From a personal standpoint, whatever you make is immediately taxed at the highest extent legally possible. This is not the case with business income.** Once all income is under this business label, all business expenses reduce income and the remaining is the net profit.

It is crucial that if we want to avoid taxation and reap the benefits of the IRS system, **we need to legally write off as many business expenses as possible**. You would be hard-pressed to do this on a personal level, hence the need for the business. Having a business credit card, business debit card, and business checking account are all essentials. **Keeping up to date with the current taxation legislation is also important.** For example, 2017 was the last year that independent contractors and small business owners could write off entertainment expenses. 2017 was also the last year before the dramatic increase in the standard deduction, which meant that charitable contributions and home mortgages don't carry hardly any weight when it comes to personal deductions. **The importance of being a small business owner as of 2018 is the ability to write off 20% of federal income taxes off of your personal AGI.** This is incredibly significant, and something many people don't attempt to utilize. Again, **the shift must be towards business deductions, and then taking the business deduction under your AGI, and then taking the standard personal deduction for the profit of what's left over, giving you three times as much ammunition to reduce federal income taxation, state income taxation, and FICA**

taxation.

5) I decreased SE/FICA taxation, legally.

Let's talk about Self-employment (SE) tax for a moment. Unfortunately, even if your only job is that of a small business owner or independent contractor, and even if you're net income is less than the standard deduction, you are STILL required to pay SE tax. SE tax is self-employment tax totalling FICA tax for social security and Medicare (7.65%) x 2 = 15.3%. **However, this seems to come out to 14.27%. This is because only 93.25% of the net income is taxed at 15.3%.**

How do we get around this? **The IRS states that as of 2019, if you DON'T have business net income > \$433, then you DON'T pay SE taxes.** That's like a standard deduction for businesses for SE tax. 433 is your base. Anything over this is deemed taxable on the entire amount. Again - it is so important that self employment net earnings does not exceed \$433. Even If it's \$434, then you are taxed around 14.26% on the entire amount, even just because of one dollar's difference. The IRS only encourages every business to show a consistent profit. Any amount > $0 of net earnings is considered a profit. Therefore, net earnings between $1 and $433 keeps us away from the focus of the IRS, while helping us to avoid SE taxes.

So, basically you have two options to make this happen. First, you could just **ensure that your business net income is always less than or equal to $433.** This is great for a small startup business where you may not have much profit yet, or even have a net loss. This is also pefect for your home business, with the home business main goal of absorbing major expenses that you would likely already personally incur (like the mortgage, utilities, etc.).

But what about the business on the side that is growing much faster than what you thought? What about the business that continues to grow year after year and make substantial profit? **You can use the S CORP**

benefits to cut SE tax amount in half or more. Wait - did I just say become and own a corporation? Being an S CORP sounds so daunting. It's not. That's because you will elect to be **treated as an S CORP.** This means you're still an LLC, but taxed like an S CORP. From an audit standpoint, as of this writing, S corporations have the lowest audit percentage of all businesses. And, as a side note, if you are not white, and not a male, but own the business, you are considered a minority and appear to be even less likely to be audited.

In order to make this happen with the S corporation, you would first file as an LLC. See my first book for an easy step by step process of creating an LLC. Then within the first 3 months of creating the LLC, you would need to elect to be treated as an S CORP. The 2 forms are on the IRS website and are easy to complete. Every new year, you have until March 21 to file again to change S CORP status. It appears like for now that it auto-renews, but I would always double check on this instead of assuming that you're forever an S CORP. What about if you have a business that you have had for years? You still can elect to be taxed as an S Corporation. You just have to do so Jan 1- March 21 of the new calendar year.

6) *Passive business investment income needs to be constantly growing.*

As taxation diminishes, refunds increase, debts are lowered, then finally profit starts increasing. The question then is what to do with it. You could keep it all in a standard savings account and make a whopping 1% in a year. Or you could do something else with it. **You could increase your cash flow with minimal risk.**

I am a huge fan of **diversifying in order to minimize risk**. As of writing this, I have a generalized investment account with **FundRise**, which is a **fractional eREIT** business that takes your money and invests in into fractions of developing/developed real estate. This process allows for safeguarding your money by further spreading in out into various projects. If this company starts to fail, then we will likely be in an economic depression, as this would be one of the last hit businesses before an economic fail. This return is about **6.19% annually**. I then have a small amount into **peer-to-peer lending** through **Prosper**, which allows a certain amount of money that you can diversify into numerous accounts to fund someone's loan through **crowdfunding**. You basically join with others to become a bank. This return is about **5.55% annually**. I also have a **traditional IRA** account with **Vanguard** focusing mostly on real estate for myself, and then High Yield Dividends and Bonds for my children and extended family. This return is about **3.29% annually.**

And then we plan on **having our businesses rent out our current home and car** for an extended amount of time while I am in medical school. The return for the rental townhome is suspected to be **31.25% annually. Though the return is significantly higher, the amount of work needed to be put into this investment is much greater**, with much less of a hands-off approach as the aforementioned passive income options. We don't plan to have more than 1 rental property before going to medical school. During medical school and residency, we plan on acquiring 1 or 2 more before graduating. After graduating, we don't plan on owning more than 5 total. After talking to other investors, **it just doesn't seem to be worth the headache to have multiple rental properties.** My view on this can certainly change, for better or for worse. We shall see.

The Lord has certainly first taught that me that the **quality of the rental home I purchase is likely to be the quality of my rental experience. If I wouldn't live in the rental property for whatever reason, why would I ever invite anyone else to come live there?** Am I purchasing a property just because it doesn't cost much initially? But then, how much money will I have to put in it throughout the rental process? Will the appliances likely die within 5 years? Is the house structurally stable? Yes, I could focus on multiple apartment complexes with numerous returns. Yes, I could focus on extremely fancy homes and rent them out to only the most extravagant travelers, via Air BnB style. But both would require significant hands-on assistance and my presence. Lower class rental properties would probably need to be fixed up constantly. And then on the other hand, Air BnB style homes have multiple temporary tenants throughout the year, inviting exponential unaccounted for variables into the situation. That sounds like a lot of headache. No thanks.

And then also- who am I inviting into this rental property? My rental experience will also depend on the tenant. For low cost rentals, the tenant may need assistance at times with the cost of rent, and may not always pay, with evictions being more prominent here. And then on the other hand, those living lavishly will likely expect the most out of the rental property and may never be satisfied with what you have to offer. **Therefore, our focus will be on the middle class, and our vetting process will certainly be drawn out in order to find the**

Dr. Grant C Davis PT DPT OCS

best match for our rental properties.

Regarding home ownership, **the first home you buy should be in your personal name.** This is because of the various low to 0% downpayment options and governmental assistance, and the taxation advantages. If you're AGI is low enough as a first time home buyer, then the state of Virginia can provide 2-2.5% down payment, pay closing costs, and give you a **mortgage credit certificate,** which is a non-refundable tax credit every year equal to 20% of yearly mortgage interest. You WANT this. If you have a spouse, you do NOT want them to co-apply for this home. This is simply because you want them to also have the same grants available when they buy their first home, as they would get all of the benefits as well. Legally, one could cosign (different than co-apply), which I would encourage every spouse to do.

Right now, I currently own our home and have deeded it to my wife upon my death. We are also in the works of trying to get another home via my wife's first home in a few years, with my wife fully owning it and deeding it to me upon her death. **The goal is clearly to not use your own money when buying things,** therefore improving your return on investment and your overall savings. This would allow us two mortgage certificate credits, which is incredibly valuable. We can then rent out each home to our rental property business for a very small amount per month, and have them rent out the properties and allow them to keep the profits. This keeps us away from having passive income personally coming our way, legally. **If you're thinking about renting out your house to yourself, do NOT do this. This is illegal.**

After completing the first home ownership, in my opinion, **I would likely never recommend buying any additional home in my personal name after the first home for myself and the first home for my spouse.** At that point, your business needs to acquire every home after your first and your spouse's first. This will save you a ton of

Dr. Grant C Davis PT DPT OCS

liability concerns and taxation issues. And lenders don't really care much about your business, except that you have the 20% down payment available upon purchase. It's actually pretty easy to get a home through your business. Many lenders don't even care where the downpayment came from. It's illegal to have the business take out a personal loan. BUT if YOU personally take out a personal loan and gift it to the business, then this is supposedly no problem. Oh the legalities...

Unfortunately, there is a surge of people doing what's called a **quit claim deed with their homes. You don't want to do this.** This is the process of acquiring a home in your personal name, and then transferring the title over to your business, and creating investment properties this way. The promises with this are three-fold: **decreased tax liability, low downpayment, and the ability to take depreciation which would lower your taxes significantly.**

Unfortunately, most of the aforementioned

stated promises aren't true. Let's start with the only true part- the downpayment. While it is true that businesses must front 20% of the loan value, and comparatively individuals now even have the 0% downpayment option, the consequences are devastating for the individual who quit claims. Allow me to explain. Many lenders have what's called a **"due on sale" clause** in their loans, stating that if the owner transfers title to someone not approved, such as the business, the lender can immediately have the original owner front the entire loan amount. The **ENTIRE LOAN AMOUNT.** People say it doesn't happen. It does. Just do your research. You do NOT want to be one of these people. Sure, you don't have to put down so much for the downpayment, but what a risk you are taking in having your bluff called, and having to front the entire loan amount. That's not worth it in my opinion.

But what if your loan doesn't have a due on sale clause? Is it still worth it? I would argue no. That's because there is the assumption that because the title is under the business name, it is liable to the business. Unfortunately, this is not true either. While it causes a little bit more work for the average Joe who would be suing you, I'm sure they wouldn't mind simply getting the **record of deed to find out who actually owns the property.** When they **see your business name on the title, but your personal name on the deed, you better believe that they will go straight for your personal belongings.** You've now opened this floodgates. This would have never happened if you had simply had the business buy the investment property first. The risk of tax liability is not worth it in my opinion.

And finally, the idea that taking depreciation will lower the tax amount due is true on the front end. **Depreciation basically covers the cost of a percentage of the home as it is being rented out.** This is given back to the owner every year, with the first year being the most refunded, and every year after that being less and less. The advantage of claiming personal rental property allows for minimal to zero self-employment tax, but then adds to federal income tax liability. You could still ensure that your federal income is virtually zero. So this sounds like a great deal, right?! The issue with this, is that **if the owner ever goes to sell the home, they are required to do back-taxes for every year of depreciation they took, for the cumulative summation of depreciation. You have to pay all of that back.** I have currently not found a way around this, though I am looking. The only option at this point may be death of ownership, and deeding it to someone else. However, that person would likely be liable for the depreciation tax. Again, not worth the risk in my opinion to quit claim deed a home.

7) Unsecured Personal loans should never be taken out.

This was something I wish someone would have told me from the very beginning. **Most personal loans are unsecured, meaning that there is no financial leverage to borrow from**. Usually secured loans are tied to assets, such as your home, or your car for example. However, if you have no equity built up in those assets, then you have nothing to borrow from. Hence, the unsecured personal loan. I had just started out in my marriage, just bought a different used vehicle, and just acquired our first home. I had nothing saved up, and no equity. We needed extra cash for our tax situation, and so I thought my only option was to get an unsecured personal loan. **It was so embarrassing.**

Here's what I should have done instead. I **should have applied for a 0% APR credit card for 14 months, and put as much as I could on the credit card. This would have bought me 14 months without any interest accruing.** I could have used cash for the bills that could not be compensated through credit. Again, this would have saved me a lot of headache, embarrassment, stress, and ultimately money.

Let's break this down from a financial standpoint. One on hand, I could take out two credit cards with 0% APR for 14 months with a combined credit amount of 20,000.

The cost for signing up? $0. Many credit cards even offer bonuses for the first 3 months of use. Comparatively, I could take out an unsecured personal loan for $20,000 and right away have to **pay 0.75 % origination costs**, leaving me with $18,500 that I can actually use. **Then the APR immediately starts, usually around 6-18% depending on your credit score, how much you take out, and your repayment length of time.** Most lenders offer 12% APR, with Citizen's Bank offering the longest length of loan life at 7 years. This is at least $200 dollars of interest every month. If you multiply that by 12 months and then by 7 for years, **you're at $16,800 for total loan interest** accrued if you pay on time every month. This means after you pay back the principal of $20,000 (with only getting to use $18,500), you would have also had to pay the interest of $16,800, **bringing the total to $36,800.**

I hope this shows how unfortunate it is to be on the receiving end of a personal loan. However, it **is very nice to be on the giving end of the personal loan**, again with organizations such as Prosper and Lending Club, that allow you to do this as low risk as possible and get a great investment return.

8) Credit cards should be paid off every month.

As I quickly learned, if your monthly debt APR % is greater than your monthly ROI %, you're not getting any where. What I mean by that, is **if you have something working against you at a greater rate than something that is helping you, you are losing financially every month.** And that's exactly what was happening to me. I wanted so badly to free myself up from any debt that I thought I needed to increase investment returns. However, the cash that I used to make that happen was not used to it's fullest, as it should have been taking out the loan or credit card with the highest rate of APR.

Credit cards are known to have insanely high % APR. It should be a no-brainer that if you own a credit card, **you want to pay off the entire balance every month.** Otherwise, most likely, interest will start accruing at an astronomical rate. This makes getting out of the chains of debt even harder. **IF you find yourself in this predicament - then you need to start a new credit card with 0% APR for 14 months and no balance transfer fee for the first 3 months**. And then obviously transfer all balances over to this card. Bank of America was flaunting this, and this is honestly a great way to shift debt and to decrease your rate of loss. Just don't forget that you need to pay it off in 14 months!

9) Debit card usage should increase for specific categories.

I am a firm believer that credit card usage is the way to go in order to have great electronic records, which makes it easy for taxation purposes, and also for the rewards associated with credit use. I use credit cards for the majority of the things my wife and I buy. However, there are several cases where it would be more advantageous to use a debit card. Let me give you two examples that deal with my personal life.

The first category where debit cards need to be used is with food. If you only allot yourself a certain amount of cash for food each month, you can't go over that limit. Your debit card will likely be rejected, and you'll penalized. This is a great limitation and safeguard, because when **Anna and I go overboard from our monthly budget, it's usually always on food and one other category.** This means when we are eating out, or even when we are going to the grocery, we need to be using our debit card.

The second category for my wife and I **involves charity.** As you might recall from my first book, I started to give all of what we had, and then more. As my wife later stated, I was giving from an empty well. It left me feeling great at the time, and then even worse afterwards, usually bitter or having some form of resentment. If I had just stayed with using my debit card, this would have never been an issue. I think sometime it's easy to give in order to desire that emotional high, especially if you're borderline depressed, which was the case for me. Giving should never be a means to feeling better about yourself. It was a hard lesson for me to learn. I still struggle with that.

10) Never buy a new car.

My dad is the one who gave me this piece of advice, and it's really great practical wisdom. As soon as the car rolls off the lot with it being purchased, it loses a great percentage of it's value. The difference between getting a used car with < 50,000 miles on it compared to a brand new car can be a difference of thousands of dollars. It's just not worth the pride and boasting.

SETTING YOUR
GOALS WITH
THE S CORP

◆ ◆ ◆

Many people live paycheck to paycheck, and say they're okay with this. The truth is, they're not. I know this, because I was one of them. There's something that happens to a person when the veil is torn and the scales fall off of their eyes. This greater awareness leaves someone in a place where they can't unsee what has been shown to them. I can never go back living paycheck to paycheck now that I know the truth about finances. And you shouldn't have to either.

1) The first goal that I have for myself and my family is to guard and protect our money.

I don't want us to starve, especially if we are working hard for something. I don't want our money stolen from us. In order prevent this, I had to learn about the taxation system. This is becoming even more crucial, as numerous presidential candidates are proposing "free" this and that for the upcoming election. The problem, is that the government doesn't make a ton of money. The United States Government is actually in debt. Trillions of dollars in debt.

So who pays for all of this free stuff, such as college, healthcare, whatever? YOU. The taxpayer. YOU. You're paying for it. And you get no say regarding what you are contributing to. Not a fan of abortion? Too bad. Not a fan of someone getting a college de-

gree in underwater basketweaving? Sorry about your luck. You don't have a choice. But wait. Yes you do. You can choose to be smarter than those who are wanting to steal your hard-earned money. You can learn how to not be taxed, legally. That for me is goal number one.

2) Goal number two is to find out how I can make more money without being penalized, hence the magical S CORP.

You may laugh at that, but the taxation category from 12% to 22% is a huge leap with no in-between numbers, and it is mostly targeted at one group of people. **The marginal tax rate has been shown to likely be the highest for the middle class AGI. For those filing single, the 22% taxation category is $39,475 to $84,200. Head of household is $52,850 to $84,200. For MFJ, it is for those that make a combined taxable income between $78,950- $168,400.** It gets capped out for the upper rich class, and is very minimal for those at the poverty line and up to 400% poverty line at around 10-12%.

This means, if your AGI falls within the middle class, the taxation system does not work in your favor. This AGI is primarily between $50,000 to $150,000. Even worse, most government subsidies and write offs fall off after 400% poverty line, as well as refundable tax credits, so most of the middle class never receive governmental benefits. That means they receive no additional help.

The rich have learned how to not pay taxes, (most of the time, legally). The poor don't have to pay taxes due to government subsidies, government write offs, and government refundable credits. **This leaves the middle class being the supporting backbone for the entire United States, and now, potentially even illegal immigrants. That's a recipe for disaster.** The poor get helped in a huge way. The rich don't need help. And then the middle class gets the shaft. They're taxed as if they were rich, and then forced to survive with much less.

So how do you make more money, and yet keep your AGI the lowest you can? You don't. You've read that correctly. You really can't. **If you want to make a killing with cash flow, you have to come to the realization that you will never be able to. But YOUR BUSINESS can!** This is why it's so important to be a small business owner. **You can write off numerous expenses, which will only doubly write off more from your "profit."**

But there is more. Let's talk about the magical S CORP. If you file as an S Corporation, you can take three major benefits: Non-Dividend Distributions tax free to you, employer provided 25% SEP retirement to the employee (you), and employer provided Health Insurance Premiums to the employee (you).

Let's start with non-dividend distributions. What is this, anway? It's a percentage of the remaining profit that is given to the owners, based on their basis. If you and/

or your spouse are the only owners, you get 100% of the distributions, tax-free. You simply take it out throughout the year or at the end of the year, marked as non-dividend distributions, and give to yourself tax-free. So why not give your entire profit to yourself through this avenue? That's because the IRS hates this and it is now deemed illegal. So how much can you take out? It depends. **First know that you will have to pay yourself part of the profit, causing an owner-employee identity. This is called a salary.** Keep this in the back of your mind as we go down the distribution alley.

This non-dividend distribution usually follows a **1/3 rule or 1/2 rule.** The 1/3 rule is generally that out of your total business revenue generated, 1/3 goes to expenses, 1/3 goes to your salary, and 1/3 goes to non dividend-distributions. **I am a bigger fan of the 1/2 rule, and this is what most court cases filed by the IRS have primarily focused on seeing.** The IRS seems to desire this equation, which is for your profit (after business expenses are deducted):

Your Salary / (Your Salary + Non Dividend Dis) $\geq$ 50%

This basically means that your salary is greater than or equal to your non-dividend distributions.

Here's an easy example. As MFJ (married filing jointly) with 2 children, let's say my LLC business makes $150,000. I write off $35,000 for general expenses and $10,000 for healthcare premiums. This leaves me with $105,000. Self employment tax on this is 93.25% of this multipled by 15.3%, **which is $14,981 in self-employment tax.**

Now let's look at federal income and state income tax. I am left with a supposed AGI of $105,000. Let's utilize the solo 401K of maximum $30,000 based on my income at this point. I am left with $75,000. This is my earned income, which means I don't qualify for the EITC. I can contribute $12,000 to my TIRA. This lowers my number to $63,000. This is my AGI. I don't qaulify for any governmental subsidies. I then deduct $24,400 standard deduction, and am left with $38,600 taxable income for federal and state. Federal income tax on this is $4,251. I apply my child tax credit of $4,000, and **I then owe $251 in federal income tax. State income tax is $2,220.** In conclusion, we ended up having to pay **$17,452 in total taxes. That's 11.63% of our gross income.** We have retirement of $42,000, and then cash flow of $45,548. To summarize:

◆ ◆ ◆

Taxes Paid: $17,452

Cash Flow: $45,548

Net Worth: $87,548

◆ ◆ ◆

That's not too bad. **Recall that this is the best compared to standard W-2 employees, abnormal W-2 employees, and even indepedent contractors.**

But let's make it even better. Now, let's take the same example of MFJ with 2 kids making $150,000 as an LLC. And now let's elect to be an S CORP. I write off $35,000 for general expenses, and then close to **$25,000 expenses for employer-donated employee benefits (I rounded it up slightly to make it easier to follow).** This includes:

-writing off 25% of my employee salary to a 401K/SEP, which counts as a business expense employer-only contribution ($11,250)

-writing off 7.65% FICA employer responsibility of my employee salary ($2,678), which again counts as a business expense, as I am also the employer.

-writing off $10,000 in healthcare premiums, which is added to the employee's wages, but not taxable medicare/SS.

This leaves me with $90,000 in profit. Half of this is $45,000. I therefore take $45,000 as my salary, and then $45,000 goes to non-dividend distributions, following the

1/2 rule. **This non-dividend distribution of $45,000 passes through tax-free to the finish line, and avoids even personal taxation.** Don't forget for the salary, the business gifted $10,000 of employee wages, though this is not part of FICA tax. That means I have $45,000 of wages, but only $35,000 of it is taxed by FICA. This employee FICA tax totals $2,768. **Total self-employment taxes: $2,768 (FICA) x 2 = $5,536.** Now we are left with federal income tax and state income tax.

Supposedly at this point, my AGI and earned income is $45,000. But this doesn't have to be true. Don't forget we can still contribute $15,000 to our 401K/SEP. **This lowers our earned income to $30,000.**

If we go further down the road of planning ahead, we know we can take 20% off of this number, due to the small business owner deduction. **This leaves us with an AGI of $24,000.** This is perfect, because this means we qualify for most government subsidies, if we need it. This also lowers our federal income taxation category to 10%. But this doesn't mean we HAVE to get taxed. Don't forget the standard deduction of $24,400, which then takes it down to $0. 0% taxation category of $0 is $0. This lowers our personal taxation liability to $0 for federal income and state income tax and opens the door for all federal refundable credits.

Recall the total $5,536 SE tax (FICA tax x 2). Now apply the refundable CTC of 2,800, and the EITC of $4,000 for MFJ with 2 children. This totals to $6,800. $5,536 SE tax - $6,800 refundable tax credits = -$1,264. This becomes $0 paid in SE tax AND $1,264 dollars refunded back to you! Not too bad! We paid $0 for all taxes, and were actually awarded a refund after all is said and done!

We have $26,250 in retirement, we have kept $45,000 of non-dividend distributions, we have a tax-free salary of $30,000, and we were refunded $1,264 for doing our tax paperwork. $45,000 + $30,000 + $1,264 = $76,264 of real cash flow. $26,250 + $76,264 = $102,514 net worth. Basically,

this says that after we paid off our $48,750 of unavoidable life expenses, we kept the rest, and we awarded an extra $1,264. This means that we kept $102,514/$101,250 = 101.24% and had to pay 0% in taxes. Congratulations.

◆ ◆ ◆

Taxes Paid: $0 (refunded $1,264)

Cash Flow: $76,264

Net Worth: $102,514

◆ ◆ ◆

So how does this compare to the previous LLC business? I'm so glad you asked:

◆ ◆ ◆

Tax Difference: LLC paid $18,716 more in taxes

Cash Flow Difference: S Corp has $30,716 more than the LLC in real cash available

Net Worth Difference: S Corp is worth $14,966 more than the LLC

◆ ◆ ◆

And then if we extrapolate this over 20 years, we get:

◆ ◆ ◆

Tax Difference: LLC paid $374,320 more in taxes

Cash Flow Difference: S Corp has $614,320 more than the LLC in real cash available

Net Worth Difference: S Corp is worth $299,320 more than the LLC

◆ ◆ ◆

What a significant difference! Don't even make me compare this to the standard MFJ couple with kids who are W-2 employees. Those numbers would be outrageous!

3) Goal number 3 is knowing how to make more money without using my own money.

This is actually very hard to do. Most of these options are not going to magically come knocking at your door. You need to look, and then when you think you're done looking, you need to keep looking. Here are the ways that I have found thus far of not using my own money to make more money.

The first is with real estate. Buying the right home in the right location at the right time can give you incredible bang for your buck, and increase your value without you having to do a thing. Our home for example was valued at $175,000 when we bought it two years ago. It is now valued at $203,000. We gained $26,000 in 2 years. That's phenomenal. All because someone valued it at a higher price than what it originally was. This means that in a year or so, we can re-finance and get a much lower mortgage monthly rate, further decreasing our expenses while only increasing in property value.

The second option is with what is called margin. This is using someone else's money for a small fee. Why would you ever want to do this? Easy. If you see a business opportunity and can make an exceptional return on investment, why not invest as much as you can? That's what margin should be used for. Robinhood offers up to $2,000 in margin (while paying a low flat monthly fee of around $10.00) to invest this in the stock market. This is how I gained $400 in one month from the stock market when only using $2,000 of my own money. However, it was very time-consuming and wasn't worth the time involved in my opinion. But again, an option to consider.

The third option would be through employee benefits with a matching 401K. It would be incredibly wise for every person to give the maximal amount that they can to their 401K every year. Not only does this ensure something available for retirement, but it decreases your tax liability significantly. There is NO reason that you should be throwing in your own money, however, without an employer match. Most employers do this, and it is certainly worth asking for this. This is free money that your employer gives just for being a part of the company. If you get a 5% employer match per year, and work 20 years for that employer, your employer has gifted you with a full year's salary, for free. Also, if you are an S Corp, don't forget about the 25% employee salary SEP employer contribution. This means is 4 years, you'd get a full year's salary in retirement. Nice!

4) The fourth goal is knowing when to focus my savings on specific investments.

Understanding various types of investments and how they fluctuate is crucial for timing a great increase in cash flow. For example, with the **stock market**, I utilize current world events, likely upcoming world events, governmental policies, GDP, economic quarterly data, and market volatility, and obviously spiritual discernment to determine when to invest and when to sell. October of 2018, I sold everything. It felt like the market was at a standstill - one day it would skyrocket, and the other day it would plummet. It was insane. I then prayed about it and sold everything. After that, the market proceeded to tank from DJI 25,000 to around 22,000, one of the sharpest declines in years.

If I had had the cash flow available, I would have certainly put all of it in the stock market at that time. Why? Because Christmas data is usually a guaranteed increase in the market. Starting the new year is usually a great way to hit the reset button with the stock market. And then governmental policies seemed to suggest that ties with China could likely improve. It was a golden time. Within 2.5 months, the stock market bounced back with an immediate U-turn. 4 months of losses returned in 2.5 months. What a great gain. This is something to always be aware of. **When the market starts tanking, you want to take notice and see if it is time to jump into the game.**

And then when the market stabilizes, you want out. Sell it all. Please note I am NOT talking about your retirement on the side. This is for personal investment by YOU. Let the smart investors handle most of your retirement. Don't touch your IRA unless you really really have to.

From what I have seen this far, investments really seem to follow the economic data. **When the stock market tanks, then most people tend to shift towards other forms of cash-flow.** Questions then start arising about the **housing market**, and people start to get nervous. **Homes that were going for higher than normal start to fall in selling price, as buyers become hesitant.** You don't want to sell an investment property when the stock market is tanking or when the economy is doing poorly. **You want to rent these homes out, even for higher rent prices than what you normally would. This is prime time to rent.** However, when home selling prices fall and buyers become weary, **look for a shift to the buyer's market. This is a great time to buy a home, especially**

when others aren't.

If you haven't noticed a trend, then you're missing it. What I have seen and what many other people seem to agree with, is that **when real estate or the stock market are not doing well, this is your moment to get more involved. When the markets are doing exceptionally well, this is your moment to get out while you can with the gain you have. Don't get greedy.**

5) Goal number 5 is keeping those in Congress who keep our taxation levels low through voting.

President Trump's Tax Cuts and Jobs Act went into affect for 2018 filing season and lasts through 2025 filing season. However, this means that it could stop going into affect if this is not renewed. Most people don't realize what good the TCAJ Act of 2018 did for the middle class. It doubled the standard deduction, which is very significant. However, if the TCAJ Act of 2018 is not re-instated or updated, the standard deduction will fall back to close to half of what it is now. This is devastating and let me explain to you why it matters so much. The standard deduction is your tax-haven or shelter from federal income and state income tax. This means that even if Congress increases the federal income taxation amount, even to 100%, if you're AGI falls under the standard deduction, you get to keep all that you have made, tax-free. That's why deductions are so important.

At any moment, Congress can get rid of federal deductions. At any moment, Congress can get rid of federal taxation credits. AND at any moment, Congress can vote on having multiple FICA taxes, or increasing FICA tax in general. As you have seen, it is so challenging and *almost* legally impossible to avoid FICA tax. But what if this was increased? And what if there were multiple FICAs? **Don't say this won't happen, because it is already happening all throughout Europe thanks to socialism.**

That's why it's so important to keep people

in the system that are less involved in big-government and are focused on keeping taxation low. Otherwise, civil unrest will be the end result. That's what happened with the Revolutionary War. Great Britain's taxation was insane. They kept adding taxes until enough was enough. This is actually why our forefathers enacted the 2nd Ammendment. And this is why the 2nd Ammendment needs to also be protected.

6) Goal number 6 is knowing how to avoid tax penalties.

Many people think that they can't avoid taxation penalities. However, Congress has written numerous exceptions in order for Congress itself to be exempt from these taxation penalties. That's why it's so important when you hear - "Oh you can't do that! You'll get penalized by the IRS! - that instead, you look for the legal way around the penalty. Let's go over an example.

Early withdrawal of money from a traditional IRA account will get you a **10% penalty that you are required to pay.** But wait - that doesn't have to be true! If you meet any of the exception criteria, you don't have to pay the penalty! What are the exceptions? Let me share specifically from the IRS:

-*"after death of the participant/IRA owner*

-*total and permanent disability of the participant/IRA owner*

-*to an alternate payee under a Qualified Domestic Relations Order*

-***qualified higher education expenses***

-***qualified first-time homebuyers, up to $10,000***

-amount of unreimbursed medical expenses (>7.5% AGI; after 2012, 10% if under age 65)

-health insurance premiums paid while un-employed

-certain distributions to qualified military re-servists called to active duty

-in-plan Roth rollovers or eligible distribu-tions contributed to another retirement plan or IRA within 60 days"

I put in bold those exceptions that are the most likely for me to utilize. Given that my family and I had some expenses with upcoming medical school, I took out a portion of our TIRA early. As you can see, will I have to pay the required 10% penalty fee? No. No, I won't. Thank you, exceptions.

7) The 7th goal is knowing when to convert your 401K and/or Traditional IRA over to a

Roth IRA.

As I just reviewed, you can certainly take out your TIRA money early before you hit the age of 59.5 years old. You want to do this, otherwise you will get forced to take out distributions after you hit this age, and the IRS will try to tax you on this amount, which is very unfortunate. The Roth-conversion is the beautiful way around this, but it has to be done incrementally. Every year prior to 59.5 years old, you want to take out a specific amount of your TIRA, and within 60 days of withdrawing it, then you want to deposit this into a Roth IRA. Then, 5 years later, you can take out this money at any moment in time, tax-free.

By doing this, you've taken advantage of lowering your current taxation income with the 401K/TIRA, and you've avoided getting taxed on this money in any way, giving you a double bang for your buck. This means if you have a $10,000 TIRA every year, and successfully roll this into a Roth IRA each year over a span of 20 years, you have avoided at least $20,000 in taxes by assuming a minmum 10% taxation category. You have also lowered your AGI by $10,000, which could potentially even put you into a lower taxation category, or if you're smart, help you to avoid getting taxed at all. **This means you save on the front end and on the back end.** What a great deal!

It is so important, however, that the amount taken out from the TIRA needs to very, very specific to how much money you are planning on earning that year. For the years that you don't earn much, or have significant medical expenses so that you can itemize a great deal, then you want to take out as much as you can from your TIRA and transfer it to the Roth IRA. For years that you make more than what you expected, you don't want to take out much from your TIRA. And if you retire early, then you can take out the standard deduction of $24,400 every year tax-free and roll that into a Roth IRA up to 59.5 years of age.

8) Goal number 8 is the benefit of being

able to give money to those that truly need it.

In my opinion, the main goal of being financially free should be in order to show the love of Jesus to the world. Most people feel loved when they receive financial assistance. I would love to be able to give my money to people that are in great need. While I am donating to charity and attempting to start a charity, I mean the goal is to have an abounding overflowing well of money that the Lord works through me to give to whomever He wants. I have so many missionary friends, and for them to make a significant impact in their communities to love people well, they need financial help. I want to get to that point to become one of those people.

BEING AWARE OF YOUR OPTIONS: FILING SINGLE

◆ ◆ ◆

What I hear from most readers is what do you do if you're single and filing taxes? **This is actually a great question and one of the most difficult issues to tackle.** If you're single, you have a very low standard deduction. Many single people that I talk to either have no kids or no longer have dependents to claim. This means no child tax credit, and hardly any earned income tax credit. So what do you do? Let me go over a big example that I hope sheds some light on the situation.

Let's say we have the standard W2 employee who makes $70,000 a year and files as single without dependents. That person would have to pay $11,345 in federal income taxes, $5,355 in FICA tax, and then $4,025 in state taxes, totalling = $15,370. $20,7525/$70,000 = 30% that this person would have to pay in taxes throughout the year.

After we do the standard deduction of $12,200, we are then taxed on $57,800. **This becomes $8,579 federal income taxes, $5,355 FICA, and $4,025 State, which is $17,959 or 26%.** If we subtract this from our total, we are left with $52,041. **Let's subtract $30,000 from expenses, and we are left with: $22,041.**

To summarize:

◆ ◆ ◆

Taxes Paid: $17,959

Cash Flow: $22,041

Net Worth: $22,041

◆ ◆ ◆

So how we do change things up? We could go the abnormal W2 employee, like from my first book, and utilize pre-tax employee benefits. We can contribute $19,000 to our 401K, and let's assume the employer offers $6,000 to our HSA and matches our contribution at $3,000. We then are left with $70,000 - $25,000 = $45,000 for income and $22,000 retirement. Let's look at taxes.

$45,000 - standard deduction $12,200 = $32,800. **Taxation liability on this is $3,742 federal income, $5,355 FICA on $70,000, and $2,588 state. $11,685/$70,000 = 16.7%. If we calculate percentage based upon cash available, we get $11,685/$45,000 = 26%. This leaves us with**

$33,315. If I subtract $30,000 in expenses, I have only $3,315 left in cash flow, but $22,000 retirement, which = $25,315 total, which is greater than the standard W2 employee, with less overall taxes paid.

◆ ◆ ◆

Taxes Paid: $11,685 (lower than normal W2)

Cash Flow: $3,315 (unfortunately lower)

Net Worth: $25,315 (higher than nornal W2)

◆ ◆ ◆

Let's see what happens when this individual owns their own company, and files this as an S CORP. They also make $70,000, and then subtract $25,000 from general expenses, $3,000 employer provided healthcare, $1,301 FICA tax employer responsibility, and gift their employee with employer contributed $699 in SEP employee retirement. This totals to $30,000 in expenses. This leaves a profit of $40,000.

They give $20,000 to themselves via non-divi-

dend distributions following the 1/2 rule, and are left with $20,000 to be their salary. They subtract $3,000 from this number for healthcare premiums paid by employer, and are left with $17,000 for FICA taxation, which is **$1,301 for FICA tax. Multiple this by 2 and we get $2,602 self-employment tax.**

Now, let's look at federal income tax and state income tax. They take the small business deduction, which lowers their $20,000 wages to $16,000 AGI. They then take the standard deduction of $11,145. This leaves them with $4,855 to be taxed on for federal income taxes and state income taxes. However, they have the saver's credit for federal, **which means $0 federal income tax. Their estimated state tax is around $360.**

They are actually awarded the EITC of $107. This lowers their overall tax amount to: $2,602 FICA + $360 state - $107 = $2,855. Total taxation: 4.08% of $70,000 or 7.31% of $40,000 cash after expenses.

This means that out of $70,000 after $30,000 of expenses are removed, this individual kept $37,145 of real cash flow, added retirement of $699, and came to $37,844 of net worth.

To summarize:

❖ ❖ ❖

Taxes Paid: $2,855 (lowest)

Cash Flow: $27,968

Net Worth: $37,968 (highest)

❖ ❖ ❖

This might not seem like a big deal, **but every year the standard W2 employee filing as single gives away $15,104 more in taxes than the small business owner that is single. Multiply this by ten years, and you have a difference of $151,040, or two year's worth of work.** That's almost like working two full years and giving it all to the IRS. This is huge! This is the difference between retiring at least two years sooner. This is the difference between investing sooner. This doesn't even account for the retirement fund growing every year for ten years.

Again, there's nothing wrong about asking your HR

person at work if it's possible to treat you as an independent contractor, and if so, then if your rates could increase. And if so, could they contract out to your business instead of specifically you. **"You don't have because you didn't ask,"** is a great paraphrase from **Jesus** that I take to heart. I would invite you to reach out and ask your employer/HR person about changing how you are paid. It really only benefits everyone. Remeber, they don't have to pay your yearly 7.65% FICA tax if you're contracted out. Think about it...

CONCLUSION

◆ ◆ ◆

I truly hope that this book was beneficial to you in a very practical way. My hope with my first book was to lay the groundwork and really highlight the benefits of different taxation identities. I hope this second book was more informative regarding the numerous pathways to choose from in order for you to save, invest, grow, and legally avoid getting your money taken from your every year.

It feels so nice to be at a much better place now than where I was two years ago. It's amazing what the Lord can do in two years of time. I'm no longer looking for a way out. I know it. I see it. And I'm starting to live it out. After medical school and residency, retirement is actually a real option. And by retirement, I mean being able to work as much as I want, when I want, with whom I want to work with, and where I want to work. That sounds so nice... And I'm grateful it's becoming more and more real.

The charity foundation is becoming more of a challenge than what Anna and I had originally intended. However, I'm hopeful that we should be finished legally creating this within the next few years. Anna has her book coming out later this year, which is very exciting! I therefore may have one more book in the works regarding taxation for amending purposes and charity formation, but for now, this may be my last, until I glean more information.

I hope to some day even venture into financial wealth advising and management. I am currently considering becoming a lawyer and specializing in taxation. Of course, this would be something I would do on the side, and this would be an option that I would consider obviously after medical school and residency are over.

People say I'm crazy. I just say life isn't meant to be boring. This idea of taking a life identification based upon your employment is very unfortunate. I am so much more than any job I will ever perform, or any act I will ever accomplish, or any achievement I will ever reach. I'm a child of God, and that makes all of the difference.

Again, I hope that this was impactful to you and your family, and I ultimately hope it encourages you to fight for the freedom that Jesus died and rose again for. You don't have to settle with the 9-5 job for 40 years. You really don't. I hope you join me on this trip! The world needs more financially independent people!

Until then, keep sharing the freedom that you've been given! In Jesus name, Amen!

REFERENCES

IRS of The United States (2019). Internal Revenue Service | An official website of the United States government. [online] Available at: https://www.irs.gov/ [Accessed 10 Jun. 2019].

PLLC, W. (2019). Colorado Springs CPA – Colorado CPA – CPA Tax Accountant. [online] Watson CPA Group. Available at: https://www.watsoncpagroup.com/ [Accessed 10 Jun. 2019].

CCH STATE TAX LAW EDITORS. (2018). U.S. Master Tax Guide 2019, 102nd Edition. Riverwoods, IL 60015: CCH Incorporated.

WELTMAN, B. (2019). J.K. LASSER'S SMALL BUSINESS TAXES 2019. [S.l.]: JOHN WILEY & SONS.

The Holy Bible. (1986). New York: American Bible Society.